STRANGE CREATURE

Michael Leunig's words and pictures were first published in Australia in 1965. He was born in Melbourne and now lives on a farm in north-eastern Victoria.

Strange Creature comprises pieces that have previously appeared in the Melbourne *Age*, the *Sydney Morning Herald*, *Nation Review*, or in various stage productions.

Also by Michael Leunig

MICHAEL LEUNIG
STRANGE CREATURE

VIKING
an imprint of
PENGUIN BOOKS

Viking
Published by the Penguin Group (Australia)
250 Camberwell Road, Camberwell, Victoria 3124, Australia
Penguin Books Ltd
80 Strand, London WC2R 0RL, England
Penguin Group (USA) Inc.]
375 Hudson Street, New York, New York 10014, USA
Penguin Books, a division of Pearson Canada
10 Alcorn Avenue, Toronto, Ontario, Canada M4V 3B2
Penguin Books (NZ) Ltd
Cnr Rosedale and Airborne Roads, Albany, Auckland, New Zealand
Penguin Books (South Africa) (Pty) Ltd
24 Sturdee Avenue, Rosebank, Johannesburg 2196, South Africa
Penguin Books India (P) Ltd
11, Community Centre, Panchsheel Park, New Delhi 110 017, India

First published by Penguin Books Australia, a division of Pearson Australia Group, 2003

10 9 8 7 6 5 4 3 2 1

Designed by George Dale, © Penguin Group (Australia)

Produced in Australia by Australian Book Connection

National Library of Australia
Cataloguing-in-Publication data:

  Leunig, Michael, 1945– .
  Strange creature.

  ISBN 0 670 04136 X.

  1. Caricatures and cartoons – Australia. 2. Wit and humour, Pictorial. I. Title.

741.5994

www.penguin.com.au

THE PLAYERS

JOHN HOWARD	Prime Minister of Australia
TONY BLAIR	Prime Minister of Britain
GEORGE BUSH	President of America
SADDAM HUSSEIN	President of Iraq
MAVIS BLOGGS	Just a person
FRED BLOGGS	Husband of Mavis; also just a person
STEVE ANVILBANGER	The award-winning newspaper columnist, who has recently been awarded the prestigious THE MOST AWARD-WINNING AWARD-WINNER OF THE YEAR AWARD
MR CURLY	Unusual, elusive and cheerful person
VARIOUS DOGS	Observers able to cope with human presence
VARIOUS DUCKS	Web-footed birds with rounded beaks; ambivalent about human presence
TEAPOTS	Simple, reliable, shared, constant consolers; can be broken
DEVILS	Charming, attractive, award-winning high achievers
ANGELS	Messengers
CARTOONS	Strange creatures of bad taste and ambiguity; feral trouble-makers and enemy sympathisers living in dark, disappointing and embarrassing holes

what can you recommend for a man who has everything but is still deeply unsatisfied ?
A War...!
GIFT ADVICE
Leunig

Strange Creature

The Australian Poly-waterpipe Ensemble

I sat beneath a shady tree,
And fearing it would fall on me,
I cut it down (pre-emptively)

I saw a little honey bee,
And fearing it would poison me,
I murdered it (pre-emptively)

I sensed a dark futility,
And fearing that it could be me,
I dealt with it (pre-emptively)

"We're all lying in the gutter but some of us are looking at the stars"
NICOLE
RUSSELL
KYLIE
Leunig

OF ALL the LOVES

OF ALL the LOVES that CAN Be known
ONE has reMained
NAMeLess;
IT'S the
LOVE of MICRoPHONE
and it's the most
ShAMeLess!

Leunig

Father, what's the difference between a column and a shaft?

A column supports something and a shaft is a regular piece of writing in a newspaper.

leunig

SHOPPING PROVERBS

- Better to have shopped and lost than never to have shopped at all.
- SHOPS WILL BE SHOPS ● Shopping is the best form of defence.
- FOOLS RUSH IN WHERE ANGELS FEAR TO SHOP ● The leopard does not change his shops ● WHEN THE CAT'S AWAY THE MICE WILL SHOP ● Shopping is the infinite capacity to take pains.
- ANY SHOP IN A STORM ● There is always room at the shop.
- SHOPPING MEN TELL NO TALES ● Shopping is stranger than fiction ● HELL HATH NO FURY LIKE A WOMAN SHOPPING.
- The husband is always lost to shop ● TO SHOP IS HUMAN.
- Shop and the world shops with you, weep and you weep alone.
- THE CUSTOMER IS ALWAYS SHOPPING ● Whom the gods would destroy they first send shopping ● WHEN THE GOING GETS TOUGH THE TOUGH GO SHOPPING ● He who hesitates is shopping.
- SHOP AND LET SHOP ● A little shop is a dangerous thing.
- SHOP AND YE SHALL FIND ● Empty shops make the most sound.
- YOU CANNOT RUN WITH THE HARES AND SHOP WITH THE HOUNDS.

Leunig

HOW TO PAY YOUR WAY AND STAND ON YOUR OWN FEET

God's grace, nature's blessings, free music from the birds — these mollycoddling handouts make us <u>SOFT</u> and <u>UNCOMPETITIVE</u>. It's time to get real and become <u>A SELF-MADE WINNER</u>!

Then it's just a matter of putting in the HOURS and the HARD WORK and watching the whole thing multiply.

First you must create your own <u>AIR</u> and <u>WATER</u>; so you will need a large, reliable chemistry set and some strong <u>STORAGE VESSELS</u>.

And until you have done all of this; and until you have spurned all those subsidies from heaven: the moonlight, the flowers, the sunrise etc. (which weaken us so), and until you have made it entirely <u>ON YOUR OWN</u>...

Then you must provide your own <u>SUNLIGHT</u> and <u>SOIL</u>; and for this you will require <u>HUGE QUANTITIES</u> of various inflammable gases and a box of matches plus a secure <u>LAVA</u> supply and machinery for crushing and <u>GRINDING</u>.

...YOU are not <u>real</u>.

Leunig

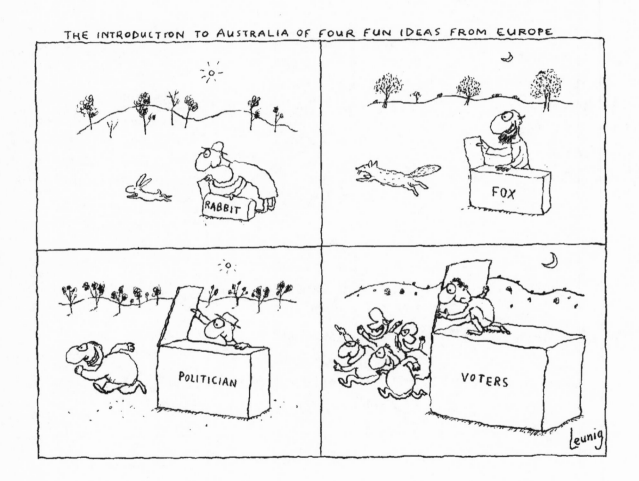

WHY DO POLITICIANS AND CIVILISATIONS FALL OVER?

Because they can no longer stand themselves.

Because they can no longer make a stand.

Because they are exhausted and want to lie down. They have stood too much.

Because they want mother to rush and pick them up and nurse them with loving tenderness and hold them for ever and ever.

Because they are top heavy and on slippery ground.

Because they need to get close to mother earth. They are _so_ tired. So very, very tired.

leunig

Father, what makes the world go around?

Money makes the world go around.

And what makes the money go around?

The money doesn't go around.

Then why doesn't the world make the money go around?

Because if the world made the money go around...

... then money wouldn't make the world go around.

leunig

Notes from the government economic think tank

The concept of the twenty-four-hour day too restrictive for retailing industry. Twenty-eight or thirty would create greater opportunity.

The matter of LANGUAGE was raised. Too regulated and socialistic. Dictionary outdated. Too much fat and dead wood. Could be broken up and privatised. Major opportunities for service providers to offer streamlined, competing alternatives for interpersonal talking.

The entire business of <u>time</u> in desperate need of DEREGULATION. The calendar and clock too unwieldy and rigid for modern economies.

HUMAN BODY SHAPE. Rationalisation overdue. If a man wants four heads why shouldn't he have them? <u>Huge</u> opportunities in dental, hairdressing, plastic-surgery industries, etc.

Law of GRAVITY discussed. Needs dismantling or restructuring. Too stifling for efficient commerce. Depresses enterprise. Too cumbersome, slow, heavy. Too evenly distributed.

THE LAWS OF NATURE generally too restrictive. Socialist conspiracy suspected. National security organisation to investigate.

Leunig

"Man is born free and everywhere he is in fast-food chains"

— ROUSSEAU (APPROX.)

Leunig

Success is
the best
revenge.

No, No, revenge
is the best
success!

leunig

BUSH
BLAIR
HOWARD
SADDAM

IRAQ...

Surprisingly, everyone who had known the killer pointed out that he had been a polite, kind and intelligent man.

a polite, kind and intelligent man.

a polite, kind and intelligent man.

a polite, kind and intelligent man.

"I think he had had enough," ... "He was in mental pain. He was screaming.

"He yelled 'Come and get me. Come and get me. Shoot me. Shoot me.' at police."

leunig

Leunig

Dear SANTA,
here's what I
want for Xmas
I WANT SADDAM!
..and if I don't get
him I'm gonna kick
your goddam fat
stupid butt with a
hellfire missile!
George.

...so we disembowel the children, decapitate the mums and dads, the dismember the old folks and then we disarm SADDAM...
GEORGE, that's Delightful.

Neil has taken a rather interesting position on the question of war with Iraq; it's the foetal position...

Leunig

... gee it's good to read about
the end of the world in a
nicely designed newspaper

leunig

... and did Tony Blair present any disturbing evidence of hidden dark forces?

Oh yes! Particularly the glint in his eye...

Person reading tea leaves — the last remaining source of reliable information. leunig

OATH OF THE DAY ... FOR THE COALITION OF THE WILLING WARMONGERS

We are the coalition of the willing warmongers.
We are powerful males.
We have war erections and brightly coloured bottoms like baboons.
We are hideous.
We stand here demanding war.

We stand here on your doorstep.
We are insurance salesmen with one foot in the door.
We are selling a policy to cover you against evil. We are selling war.
We stand here and we stand here.
We will not go away.
We have erections.

We stand here obsessed with power.
Our lives have been dedicated to the pursuit of power.
Our vision has been shaped by this lifelong obsession.
Some say the glass is half empty.
We say the glass is half full of poison.

We are the willing warmongers.
We are willing to declare war.
We are willing for others to do the fighting, the killing, the dying.
We are the good guys.
We have erections and brightly coloured bottoms.
We are unbelievably hideous.

Leunig

Summer Diary

Today we got a letter from the Americans. They say our family isn't doing enough about terrorism. They say we're too slack and disorganised. But heaven's above — it's summer!

They are threatening to take control unless we clean up our act. Not easy for a family whose motto is, "Live and let live"

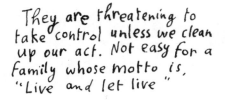

We've made a bit of an effort to instill some fear in the children but they just laugh at us and tell us to relax.... Fair enough.

The dog absolutely refuses to growl at strangers. Instead he just licks them. How slack is that ?!

Sure, the garden's a bit overgrown which provides concealment opportunities; but we like it that way — it brings the birds; we hide in it ourselves. It's nice!

We're supposed to report any unusual activities. The fact is, we've never known anything else. We like "unusual". We thrive on it. Christmas eve is our deadline. We're trying to get the dog up to speed but it's not looking good.

leunig

Summer diary

Last night I had an amazing dream. I dreamed I was an American and I could do anything I wanted and nobody could stop me.

I could do anything I wanted but I couldn't enjoy it because people kept staring at me and whispering amongst themselves.

The trouble was that whenever I started doing something I then discovered that I wasn't wearing any trousers.

I was all powerful but all insecure and worried and unsatisfied. What a rotten dream!

I would try to pull my shirt down to cover myself but it was too short. How humiliating!

I woke in a cold sweat to discover that I was just an ordinary Australian dickhead — but with a pair of trousers. What a relief.

Leunig

Father, what's the
difference between "a just
war" and "just a war"?

"A just war" is one
which is being planned
and "just a war" is one
which has already happened.

Greater love hath no man than this: that he lay down his life for a friend of mine.

...this anti-Americanism
is destroying
the world...

We can fix that!
We'll go out and
promote America
really hard !

That's what caused
the problem...

Leunig

There is a missile, so I've heard
Which locks on to the smallest bird;
Finely tuned to seek and kill
A tiny chirp or gentle trill.

It's modern warfare's answer to
An ancient wisdom tried and true:
When fighting wars you first destroy
All songs of innocence and joy.

leunig

The mother
of all bombs.

The mother
of two girls
and one boy.

Leunig

A SHORT HISTORY OF EXPLOSIONS

Explosions were invented by the Chinese many centuries ago.

The English particularly liked the idea, developed it, built an empire on it and grew rich.

The Americans, however, made explosions into a sophisticated science. America has made more numerous, more huge and more complex explosions than any nation on earth. On the Hollywood screen and in other people's homelands, America has filled the world with explosions.

Now explosions are affordable, accessible and reliable. You can get them anywhere.

leunig

The SMILING ASSASSIN.

The gentleman who developed the cluster bomb.

The person who designed the hellfire missile.

The inventor of the new, improved napalm.

The guy who dropped the daisy cutter.

The man who ordered the invasion.

leunig

... and very soon we'll be observing the birth of a special, dear little baby in Bethlehem and also the killing of many, many special, dear little babies in Iraq...

Leunig

Mr War
has been released
and is billeted
at our house.

He stands in
the corner and
stares at us while
we eat our dinner.
It's difficult to talk
or relax. He has
a nasty smell.

When we go to bed
Mr War stands in
the dark hallway
and we hear his
strange hard irregular
breathing all night.

The next morning
the smell is right through
the house but we can't
see Mr War anywhere.
The heater won't
work. A picture has
fallen off the wall.

It doesn't feel like
home any more. We
hear a strange rubbing
rasping noise up in
the ceiling. Everyone
feels a bit miserable
and uneasy.

We find Mr War's
boots and trousers
in the fridge. There
is a loud thumping
sound in the bathroom.
We don't know how
long Mr War is staying.

Leunig

Mr War, our unwanted, uninvited house guest, shows no sign of leaving. What a morbid presence.

He is having a strange disturbing effect on our home. We are bickering a lot. Relationships are troubled.

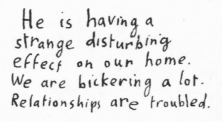

Mr War has a huge, seething intensity but offers no meaning or sense. From the darkness of the next room he will suddenly cry out something like "BANG!" in a violently loud, ugly and demented voice.

Then silence. Later, a short snuffling laugh, a low growl, the quick squeaking of leather in the dark. A squalid disillusioning sense of shame, loneliness and confusion fills the home.

Yesterday Mr War left photographs in odd, prominent places all through the house; sordid sickening pictures of cruelty, savagery, blood and death.

We were shaken and distressed and deeply saddened. "BANG!" cried Mr War from the blackness of his room. And then his horrible snuffling.

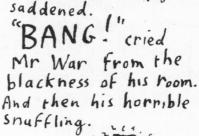

Leunig

And here we have the honey bee who carries pollen from flower to flower, bringing life and fertility to the seeds...

... and taking the fresh, fragrant nectar to create honey which brings health and sweetness to life.

And there we have the predator drone: a pilotless, remote-controlled aircraft which fires Hellfire missiles at suspects to shred and incinerate their lives into nothingness.

Dear little bee, you'll have to work much harder.

Leunig

Letter from the REAL World

" ... our community is holding a series of fundraisers to support the forthcoming military strike against the enemy.

Several cake stalls and a lamington drive have been conducted with great success.

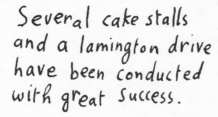

A carwash and sausage sizzle will be held on Saturday at the scout hall to coincide with a walkathon. Let's hope it's a nice day.

We are sponsoring a land mine. The Defence Department has sent us a photograph of it. The photo is displayed on the noticeboard at the local supermarket. It's a nice beige colour.

Our landmine has the serial number: DD-22BV1782/01 but we have named it "Bubby" because somebody described it jokingly as "an ankle biter."

We will receive reports of Bubby's progress and be informed of any sudden developments."

Leunig

" Already some bad news about 'Bubby', the landmine our community is sponsoring in the impending war against the enemy.

Apparently Bubby was positioned outside a defensive perimeter but was dug up and stolen in the night by an unfriendly local warlord and repositioned in an unknown location.

The Minister for Defence has informed us that due to a misunderstanding, landmine number DD-22BV1782/01 (Bubby) will not be able to serve in the forthcoming conflict.

This is due to the fact that army records show that it was deployed last year in a different theatre of war which shall remain nameless.

There is much consternation in our community as to whether we should continue supporting Bubby who really _has_ 'given legs', to our community spirit. It's all getting quite complicated.

This is a difficult one. We have become quite bonded to our landmine and next weekend a prayer vigil will be held for Bubby's safe return in one piece..."

Leunig

War Diary

The modern soldier is Hi-Tech which means he is GOOD and RIGHT. POWER IS TRUTH...

...as we all know.

The SOLDIER CAN see in the dark and is ORGANISED AND can call in MASSIVE AIRSTRIKES INSTANTLY!

The CIVILIAN is made of FLESH which is Flawed and VULNERABLE and that's ALL WRONG AND DISGUSTING

Hooray for the YOUNG SOLDIERS and their BRAND NEW EQUIPMENT. HOORAY for the great big army so strong and CERTAIN with it's amazing SHINY MEDALS and UNIFORMS.

And furthermore, the civilian CANNOT SEE IN THE DARK and doesn't know what to do. HOW WORTHLESS

SHAME, BOO and HISS to the weak civilians who can't even call a sparrow down from the sky. CIVILIANS ARE WET. WISHY-WASHY LOSERS...

...and they know NOTHING!

Leunig

ERRORISM...
We're really VERY SORRY
about this. We're actually
GOOD people - extremely
decent and CIVILISED...
THIS is just one of those
terrible, unfortunate MISTAKES
for which we APOLOGISE.
Leunig

You're too late! The stable is burned, the baby is dead, the mother and father are killed — the shepherds, the donkey, the animals, the angel... ALL DEAD! ALL ASHES!
Leunig

Into the hidden caves of ordinary life the people withdraw to take shelter...

... to light their secret home-made candles and to talk amongst themselves about the war...

... about America, about Afghanistan, the tragedy, the mess, the President's address. And they express forbidden thoughts, and furthermore...

... forbidden sympathies and doubts and dark suspicion. They listen to the sacred, outrageous voice of intuition.

Outside, the images and words rain down upon the land. The official story pounds the surface of their lives.

But in the people's secret caves and catacombs — behind their eyes, beneath their homes — creativity and life goes on; elaborate, vast and interconnected. The truth cannot be captured. It is too well protected.

Leunig

Here's the man with the sweetest heart
Who pulled the bomb on the tiny cart;
The bomb that fell
 Beside the well
Where crouched the girl
With the little curl
And the dearest sweetest heart–o.

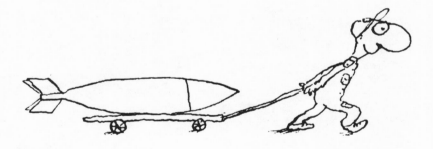

Leunig

Steve Anvilbanger, <u>AWARD-WINNING</u> columnist, gets tough on peaceniks.

" The wet elites and the bleating liberal peaceniks are on the run — a confused broken rabble of sickening wimps. WELL DAMN THEM!"

" America will do whatever it takes to make sure there is never another September eleven."

" Even if it means changing the calendar and having September ten twice and then moving straight on to September twelve. The bleeding hearts can go to hell."

Maybe I shouldn't mix the whiskey and the viagra together before I work. It could be a deadly cocktail.

Leunig

A Christmas Pudding

Take one cup each of hope, innocence, beauty and wisdom. Mix gently.

Blend in the yolks of seven big, fat fear-mongering lies.

Squeeze the juice from some old clichés about mateship, war, security, evil and freedom.

Finely chop a large bunch of fresh newspaper columns and use as garnish for dead rat.

Mix ingredients and shape into a rounded lump, having carefully removed rat.

Hurl lump at nearest wall and cry out joyfully, "PEACE ON EARTH, MERRY CHRISTMAS AND A HAPPY NEW YEAR!" etc.

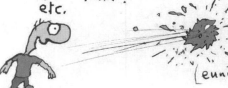

Leunig

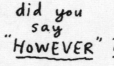

The september eleven terrorist attacks were evil and tragic, however...

did you say "HOWEVER"?

You are charged with howevering. How do you plead?

I THINK I WAS SUFFERING FROM TEMPORARY INDIVIDUALITY.

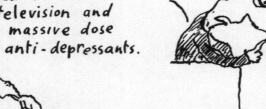

I order that you be taken from this place to a stainless-steel chamber where you shall be strapped to a chair in front of a television and administered with a massive dose of hamburgers and anti-depressants.

The war against Howeverism could take years but we are patient people and we will win... MAKE NO MISTAKE!

Leunig

Your anti-Americanism is so blatantly obvious...

Leunig

Ah yes! Very impressive!
Computerised, hi-tech, state-
of-the-art can of worms!

Leunig

Have some democracy...
we've got lots to spare we
don't use any more...

Leunig

War Against Terror — the logo

Here is the logo

Here is the T-shirt

Here is the Fragrance

Here is the shoulderbag

Here is the store
There are the customers
There is the merchandise

PLUS

The CARD
The SHAREHOLDERS
and...
The LIFESTYLE

Leunig

Why did you attack
me? WHY!!
I'll tell you why...
because you envy my
prosperity and my freedom!

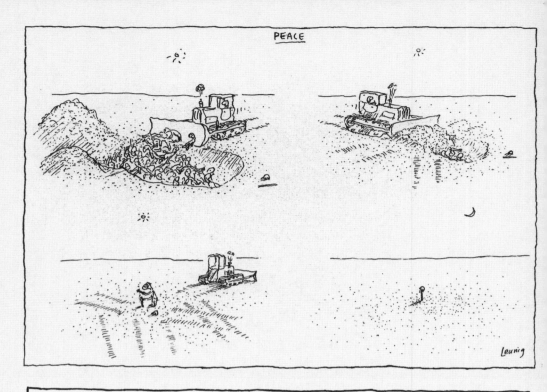

GALLIPOLI COCKATOO

As a fledgling she was rescued from her broken nest and taken in by soldiers who were training by the Goulburn River.

As a mascot she was smuggled to Gallipoli where, in the trenches, she learned to swear and raise her crest in the darkest, most miserable moments.

She reminded the boys of home: of freedom, innocence and the great spirit. She witnessed the misery of war and great suffering and courage in the face of an impossible situation.

She was taken back to Australia and lived in many homes with many keepers. The years passed and she stared brightly and deeply through the bars of her cage and through the meanness and madness of human society.

She saw the world grow faster and louder and harder. She would raise her crest and swear and try to remind them of home and freedom and the great spirit but people were too busy and faithless to understand the wisdom of an old cockatoo.

By the 1990s she found herself caged as a novelty outside a pet shop in a busy suburban shopping centre where shoppers mocked her wretched condition as they struggled for bargains and parking spaces.

Then a young boy named Ted began to visit her. His eyes sparkled with the great spirit and she raised her crest to him. One afternoon he arrived with wire cutters and quickly set to work on her prison.

She clambered to freedom and rose into the evening sky and as she set her course for the old river she looked down to see the small boy being led away to face a very difficult situation.

Leunig

A MESSAGE FROM THE PRIME MINISTER OF AUSTRALIA

My fellow Australians,

There have been reports that my anti-terror fridge magnets have lost their grip, are not holding and are slipping and sliding. I am therefore mailing to every household in Australia some special anti-terror sticky tape and some anti-terror glue so that the fridge magnets can be made more secure. Security is my passionate concern. Until your anti-terror adhesives arrive I suggest that you lay your fridge on its back in a horizontal position on the floor which will allow the anti-terror magnet to remain properly positioned on the fridge door.

Advance Australia Fair!

and keep smiling, John.

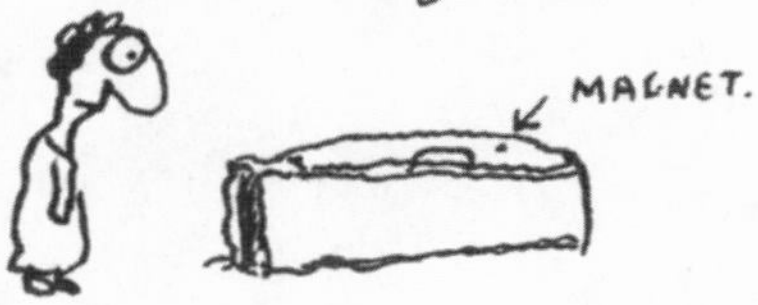

Leunig

Mr Curly transports wayfaring pilgrims away from the bad mood of the world to the peaceful shores of Lake Lacuna, a small, mystical and beautiful place of sanity which lies between the large, uncontrollable forces, the great powers and the major issues. The little goat-drawn cart has been carved from a huge potato.

Leunig

Men of Steel Q & A

Q. Why steel?

A. Steel will not burst from inner pressure
   or collapse because of an internal vacuum.

Q. What inner pressure?

A. Murderous rage.

Q. What internal vacuum?

A. Radical shame.

Q. How is shame evident?

A. The pursuit of congratulations and the
   practice of self-congratulation.

Q. How is murderous anger evident?

A. Excessive 'them and us' talk. Excessive
   talk of 'military victory' while wearing
   a lurid grin. Excessive love of power.

Q. Are men of steel immune from war-
   crimes prosecution?

A. They are already enclosed by steel walls.
   Punishment enough.

The FULL unedited AUSTRALIA day OATH

WE ARE AUSTRALIAN
WE don't quite under STAND what's going on HERE
consequently some blokes have resorted to doing browneyes in public, quite
PROUDLY. Now that's pretty BRAVE. STRONG
language is used. A situation of OPEN slather prevails AND
being alcohol TOLERANT helps enormously. So WE
STAND HERE, and all things being EQUAL, where
else can we stand? That's FAIR enough, surely. Standing here is a tried and
TRUE activity; AND it's FREE. Stringing words TOGETHER is
more difficult so WE WILL probably have to BUILD some more schools
at some stage in THE FUTURE, but chances are WE WILL NOT.
So forget the future, FORGET THE PAST, WE WILL just STAND
TOGETHER. WE ARE AUSTRALIAN.

leunig

...I love her far horizons
I love her jewel-sea
Her beauty and her terrorists —
The wide brown land for me!

HOW TO DEAL WITH A TERRORIST ATTACK

In the next few weeks you will probably be confronted by a terrorist so here's what to do.

The FULL NELSON wrestling hold is probably still the most effective means of dealing with the most determined attacker.

You must quickly leap behind your opponent, place your arms under his armpits and join your hands behind his neck.

Now exert pressure with your hands, forcing him to bend over.

Still maintaining the pressure, ride up on his back and call upon him to give up or desist. He will probably do so.

If the terrorist is defiant or fails to respond, keep him bending over until assistance arrives.

Leunig

Terrorism blows you up.

Nastiness grinds you down.

Stupidity wears you out.

Media sucks you in... ...drags you under.

Politics does you over.

Up, down, in out, under, over! But ducks... ducks just LET YOU BE.

Leunig

Sorry sir but under air-safety regulations your upper left canine tooth is too pointy for security clearance and we cannot permit you to travel on the aircraft...

leunig

our way of life is
being threatened by
a dark force.

we must defend our
way of life.

WHAT IS THIS
DARK FORCE WHICH
THREATENS OUR WAY
OF LIFE ?

it's our way
of life...

leunig

Father...
what are
terrorists ?

I'm not sure
but we used
to call them
guerillas or
partisans or
freedom fighters.

We used to
call them Robin
Hood and his
merry men ...

Leunig

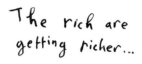
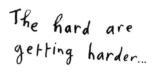

Evil celebrity, Saddam Hussein
You have touched my inner pain
And turned it into virtue;
How I'd LOVE to hurt you
And crush you, if I could;
You make me feel SO GOOD
For when I see the badness in your picture
My goodness feels SO MUCH RICHER.
I hate you, I hate you, Saddam Hussein;
Again and again and again and again
And again and again
And again!
And in a way
This keeps my chin up.
Saddam, you are my pin-up.

Leunig

Summer Diary

Yesterday, normality was supposed to return but it didn't.

"it's not coming back," said a man in the street, "It's all finished, kaput!"

"They've stopped making it," said the lady in the shop, "discontinued! people weren't using it, too slow!"

"There was no such thing as normality," said a smart-looking fellow. "it was all a bloody lie." He was so sure of himself.

I believed in it, although I couldn't really prove it existed — nor could I describe it very well...

... except to say that it seemed to hold everything together, more or less.
Anyway I'm going to miss normality for the time being but I'm not giving up hope. I <u>need</u> it.

Leunig

WE HAVE MOVED

We have moved.
At least we feel
like we've moved.

But if we have
we don't know
where to.

We seem to have
shifted. EVERYTHING
seems to have shifted.

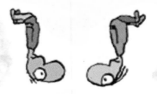

How would we know?
We can't believe anything.
We can't keep up.

And we can't keep down.
Down isn't where it
used to be, and up
is now sideways.

We've moved.
Everybody, everything
has moved.
But not the dog.
Of course not.

Leunig

The interesting thing about terrorism is that the more you think about it, the more normal it seems... Why is that?

But the Prime minister; the more you think about him, the weirder he seems. Why is that?

Leunig

Doctor, I've got a feeling.

You poor thing, tell me all about it.

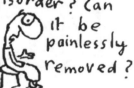

It's a little pang of lonely sorrow. Do you think it's a personality disorder? Can it be painlessly removed?

It could be LHS: Live Human Syndrome.

It's affecting my eyes. They've developed a sad, disillusioned, exiled, abandoned look.

And tell me, do you believe in the war against terror?

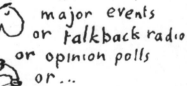

No I don't. And I don't believe in kylie or the great global promise or the boom economy or supermarkets or major events or talkback radio or opinion polls or...

That's it. You've got it. You've got LHS...

Leunig

Keep moving...
Keep moving...
Everybody keep moving!
Hurry along
Keep a move on
Hurry up, keep going...
No time to linger
Move along now.
Find something new.
Stop brooding... move on...
Don't look back.
No hanging about. Keep moving...!
Leunig

And you will find a lowly stable and a baby lying in a manger...
...and you will take control of the situation and impose security measures...
...and you will sanitise and disinfect everything and get rid of the animals which are a health risk...
...and you will gather statistical data and connect the electricity and install central heating...
...and you will introduce democracy and teach the parents to better themselves in a new global economy.
And you will show the child how to invest and be a winner with positive attitudes and good contacts and good ADVICE...
...and if they Resist...
...if they resist, call this number ...report the situation...
...and wait until a team of experts arrive.
So long as lowly stables exist there can be no peace on earth...
Leunig

For christmas he got <u>nothing</u>.

And what a beautiful, sad, lonely, little nothing it was.

He carried it around all day long and played with it.

He was so absorbed in it that he began to cry and cry and cry.

By the next morning it was completely worn out and had fallen apart.

Life would return to normal. Almost. There was a funny faint memory of the sad, beautiful, lonely little nothing.

leunig

The people
are disillusioned
with the political
process.

The people are
disillusioned with
politicians.

The people are
disillusioned with
the people !

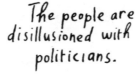

The people are
disillusioned with
themselves !!

The people are
irritable.
The people are
cranky.
Life isn't all
that it was cracked
up to be.
The people are disillusioned.

Something is missing.
WHAT CAN IT BE ?

The people haven't
got tails to wag.

Leunig

A STATE PREMIER

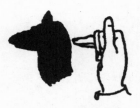

A PRIME MINISTER

A JOURNALIST

A PARKING OFFICER

A CRITIC

YOURSELF

Leunig

DAFFODILS

I wandered lonely as a cloud
That floats on high o'er vales and hills
When all at once I saw a crowd,
Not a bit like daffodils;
Beside the lake, beneath the trees,
Politicians, if you please!

Not any likeness, could I say,
They bore to flowers, that welcome spring
Their clothes were blue and charcoal grey;
It was a most depressing thing;
So off I wandered through the hills
In search of golden daffodils.

Leunig

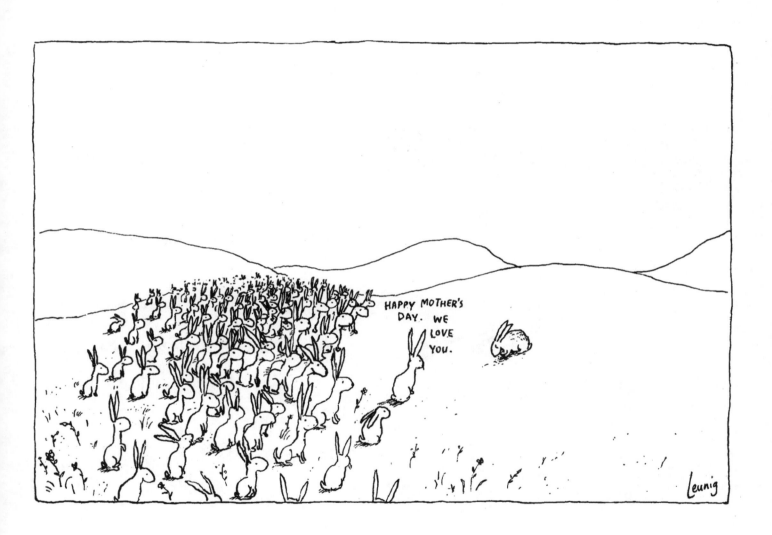

You can lead a horse to water
But you can't make it cheerful;
The bucket is full
But the horse is tearful
So you give it a loving earful.
"What's up old fellah?" you say.
He looks at you and looks away.
Of course:
The dear old inner horse.

Leunig

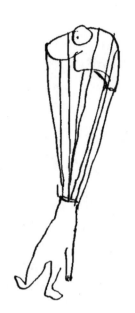

Leunig

The GREAT AUSTRALIAN GREETING

THE AUSTRALIAN GREETING "HOW ARE YOU GOING, MATE?" ORIGINATED IN SYDNEY AMONGST MALE CONVICTS OF THE FIRST FLEET. IT WAS NOT A GREETING IN ITS ORIGINAL FORM, BUT A QUERY RELATING TO THE SHORTAGE OF "AVAILABLE" WOMEN.

How are you going to mate?

Damned if I know. How are you going to mate? Perhaps we can improvise.

THROUGH WEARINESS AND INDIFFERENCE THE "TO" WAS SOON DROPPED AND THE QUERY BECAME A COMMON UTTERANCE OF GRIM RESIGNATION: "HOW ARE YOU GOING, MATE?" — A TIRED, MINDLESS RITUAL ACKNOWLEDGING A SHARED BURDEN OF FRUSTRATION AND MISERY.

THE second most frequently asked question in the colony related to the anticipation of death.

How are you going?

I've given up hope of going peacefully in my sleep so I might throw myself off a cliff. How are you GOING?

THESE FRANK AND DISTURBING QUESTIONS PASSED INTO POPULAR LANGUAGE DISGUISED AS BANAL GREETINGS. TO THIS DAY AN UNDERLYING, FORLORN RESONANCE EVOKING DEATH AND LONELINESS IS USUALLY PRESENT IN THE VOICING OF THESE GREETINGS — IN SPITE OF GLIB DELIVERY.

OWYAGOIN MATE

OWYAGOIN

currently there appears to be a revival of the questions in their original forms and with their original meanings.

HOW ARE YOU GOING TO MATE?

I'D RATHER TALK ABOUT HOW I'M GOING BECAUSE I'VE THOUGHT ABOUT IT A LOT LATELY.

Leunig

We need a
new defence force
which is small, quick,
clever and efficient.

Have we
considered
a large pack
of fox
terriers
sir?

We **have**
considered the
fox terrier
option...

and...?

and splendid though
they are in battle; obedient and
disciplined — courageous in
deportment and deed...

yes sir...

Alas, on ceremonial occasions,
they cannot manage a
slow march. Their feet
move too quickly. An
absolute
fiasco. A
total farce.
A complete
cock-up.

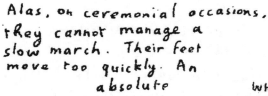

what a
pity
sir.

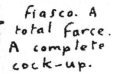

leunig

Father's Day Gift Catalogue

MOBILE PHONE – SHAVER.
Now dad can shave and attend to those important calls as he drives to work.

TRIBAL DRUM WITH EMAIL FACILITY.
Now dad can access those vital business messages while he's connecting to the lost tribe of his soul and following his bliss.

SAXOPHONE TELEVISION WITH CORDLESS ELECTRIC DRILL.
Now dad can watch current affairs, play the blues and attend to those odd jobs around the house.

WRAPAROUND SUNGLASSES WITH CONCEALED TEAR CATCHERS AND REAR DOWNPIPES.
Now dad can cry without anybody noticing.

The FESTIVAL of QUIET RESIGNATION

Winter approaches. The season of FESTIVALS is almost finished. You go to one of the last: "THE FESTIVAL OF QUIET RESIGNATION".

"I might as well," you mumble to yourself.

You arrive. Nobody much has bothered to turn up but the general feeling of quiet resignation is strong. A plastic bag blows along the ground yet nobody takes any notice.

The main attraction is a mirror leaning against a brick wall. You stand and stare at yourself with quiet resignation.

It begins to rain so you walk about in the rain with quiet resignation.

There is a barbecue but the gas bottle is empty. "C'est la vie," says the man with quiet resignation.

As you leave you see a member of the organising committee sitting in a broken plastic chair. "What else would you expect these days?" he murmurs to nobody in particular. "Fair enough," you think to yourself.

Leunig

THIS WEEK'S
FOOTY TRIBUNAL

THE SNAKE

GETS

ELEVEN WEEKS !

Western Dingos ruckman, Wayne McSnakey, was suspended for two weeks for racial abuse against Northern Reptiles rover, Abdul El Fatwami Zadish Kahloohn.

Found guilty of the charge of lying on top of Reptile's half-back, Alan Smoothie, in a degrading and bestial manner for an excessive period of time, McSnakey received a further two-week suspension.

On a charge of spiritual and emotional abuse using his index finger against Reptiles forward, Bill Smith, McSnakey was rubbed out for a further two matches.

On a charge of thirty-two counts of licking Reptile centre man, Bob Spool's, neck, McSnakey was found guilty and rubbed out for one week.

As a result of being charged with one count of pinning and fifty-seven counts of pelvic-thrusting Reptile winger, Bob "The Ferret" Burrow, McSnakey was scrubbed for an additional three games. Two counts of pelvic-thrusting were not proved.

On a charge of grabbing the umpire's whistle, dropping it into his jock-strap and suggesting in a lewd manner to umpire Brian Bean that he "come 'n' get it," McSnakey was ordered to undertake counselling.

Leunig

Leunig

Twelve important, good-natured human types currently being shamed, persecuted or devalued in the heartless new world order of systems and efficiencies.

① The GALOOT

② The DUMBCLUCK

③ The SILLY BILLY

④ The Dingbat

⑤ The BOOFHEAD

⑥ THE Wally

⑦ The BIRDBrain

⑧ The Duffer

⑨ The GOOSE

⑩ The Simpleton

⑪ The Bumpkin

⑫ The common Dunderhead

Leunig

'Quick, Beryl, come and see – it's a helmeted honeyeater'

Good King Wenceslas looked out, on the feast of Steven:
One meat pie with lots of sauce, heated all uneven.
"Where's your manners?" Steve cried out, as the pie was cooling.
"How can I relax and eat, while you sit there droo-ooo-ling."

A Quick guide to Six Common Australian Uncles

Uncle Dick:

an uncle Dick is often a bit scruffy and untidy but he's mostly in a good mood and is very loveable.

Uncle RON:

Uncle RONs are known for their odd opinions and astonishing theories about life; they're a bit of a worry yet they have such sweet natures.

Uncle KEN:

Uncle Kens can be terrible know-alls and a bit bossy but they actually are clever and generous and really nice deep down.

Uncle BRIAN:

An uncle Brian is usually playing tricks and pranks and can be an exasperating dork but they're truly wonderful when all is said and done.

uncle FRANK:

Uncle Franks are famous for being earnest and disapproving and yet, in the main, they have hearts of gold.

Uncle BoB:

An uncle BoB is inclined to be extremely embarrassing — they simply don't know when to stop; but you have to love them because they're so cuddly and gorgeous!

Leunig

The Most Terrible Coffee Table Books of Tuscany, etc.

A YEAR IN A MENTAL HOSPITAL IN PROVENCE

The Angle Grinders of ALSACE

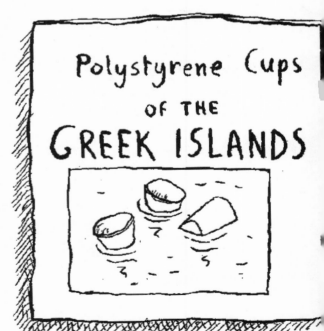

Polystyrene Cups OF THE GREEK ISLANDS

The TOW TRUCKS OF *Tuscany*

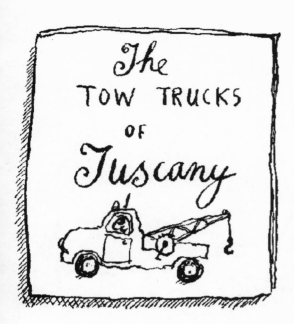

PARKING METERS OF THE *Loire Valley*

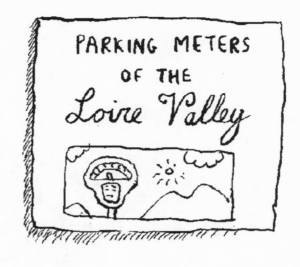

SECRETS FROM THE PRISON KITCHENS OF NORMANDY

THE MOST PHOTOGRAPHED, VISUALLY CLICHÉD LAVENDER FARMS, VINEYARDS AND OLIVE GROVES OF THE CÔTE D'AZUR

DAWKS FOR WAR or PEACE DEPENDING ON THE WAY THINGS TURN OUT

Shower rage.

PARIS ROME LONDON

ACCIDENTAL BOMBING FOR DUMMIES